PARIS
THEN & NOW

PARIS. — La Rue de   ND Phot

PARIS
THEN & NOW

PETER AND ORIEL CAINE

THUNDER BAY
P·R·E·S·S

San Diego, California

This book is dedicated to all inspiring teachers, especially Annemarie Hollis.

Thunder Bay Press
An imprint of the Advantage Publishers Group
5880 Oberlin Drive, San Diego, CA 92121-4794
www.thunderbaybooks.com

Produced by PRC Publishing Limited,
The Chrysalis Building, Bramley Road, London W10 6SP, U.K.

An imprint of **Chrysalis** Books Group plc

All notations of errors or omissions should be addressed to Thunder Bay Press, Editorial Department, at the above address. All other correspondence (author inquiries, permissions) concerning the content of this book should be addressed to PRC Publishing Limited, The Chrysalis Building, Bramley Road, London W10 6SP, U.K.

ISBN 1-59223-136-5

Library of Congress Cataloging-in-Publication Data available on request.

Printed in Taiwan

1 2 3 4 5 07 06 05 04 03

ACKNOWLEDGMENTS
The authors would like to thank the staff of le Musée Carnavalet, la Bibliothèque Historique de la Ville de Paris, la Photothèque des Musées de la Ville de Paris, les Archives Nationales, la Bibliothèque Mitterrand (Bibliothèque Nationale de France), and la Bibliothèque des Arts Décoratifs.

The publisher wishes to thank the following for kindly supplying the photographs that appear in this book:

"Then" photography
© Photothèque des musées de la Ville de Paris/Cliché: Degraces for pages 60, 62, 66, 86, 92, 96, 114, 116; © Photothèque des musées de la Ville de Paris/Cliché: Joffre for pages 20 (main and inset), 28, 34, 52, 68, 70, 90, 104, 118, 120, 134, 138, 140, 142; © Photothèque des musées de la Ville de Paris for pages 26, 44 (inset), 50, 76, 106; © Photothèque des musées de la Ville de Paris/Cliché: Pierrain for pages 94, 128, 136; © Photothèque des musées de la Ville de Paris/Cliché: Jean-Marc Moser for page 32; © Photothèque des musées de la Ville de Paris/Cliché: Ladet for pages 6, 8, 40, 44, 48, 56, 64, 74, 78, 88, 102, 112, 122; © Photothèque des musées de la Ville de Paris/Cliché: Lifermann for pages 24, 108, 126; © Photothèque des musées de la Ville de Paris/Cliché: Andreani for pages 12, 16, 36, 38, 58, 72, 80; © Photothèque des musées de la Ville de Paris/Cliché: Briant for pages 22, 42, 46, 84, 98, 100, 110, 124, 132; © Photothèque des musées de la Ville de Paris/Cliché: Habouzit for pages 18, 30, 54, 82, 104 (inset); © Photothèque des musées de la Ville de Paris/Cliché: Toumazet for pages 10, 14. The photograph on page 130 was kindly supplied courtesy of Peter Caine.

"Now" photography
All photographs were taken by Simon Clay (© PRC Publishing Limited), with the exception of the photograph on p. 7, which was supplied by © Paul Thompson; Eye Ubiquitous/CORBIS.

For cover photo credits, please see back flap of jacket.

All inquiries regarding images should be addressed to Chrysalis Images.

Pages 1 and 2 show: the crossroads of St André des Arts and Bucci now (photo: © Photothèque des musées de la Ville de Paris/Cliché: Briant), and today (photo: © Simon Clay (© PRC Publishing Limited)); see pages 100 and 101 for further details.

INTRODUCTION

One of the key moments in the history of Paris, clearly illustrated in the pages of this book, is the incredible rebuilding of the city in the middle of the nineteenth century. In 1852, when Napoleon III became emperor, the city that he inherited as his capital was far from prestigious. Political revolution had delayed the improvements brought about elsewhere by the industrial revolution. While other European cities were enjoying the elegance of avenues, the convenience of public transportation, the comfort of sewers, and the splendors offered by opera houses, theaters, parks, and gardens, Paris had hardly moved on since the Middle Ages.

By 1852 the capital was suffocating from massive overcrowding. Its population had doubled since the Revolution. The streets were heavily polluted, and there were only the most rudimentary of drains, which simply channeled filth into the Seine. Parisians were still emptying sewage and waste into the streets, allowing it to drain into the river from which they were getting their drinking water. In 1832 there had been a massive cholera epidemic in which 20,000 people died.

Napoleon III would change all of this. In less than two decades, 70 percent of old Paris had disappeared. One of history's most spectacular urban projects had transformed Paris from a disease-ridden slum into a beautiful, elegant capital. A small team of men was able to turn the confusion and chaos of Paris into a city of unity, harmony, and architectural symmetry. Napoleon III entrusted the rebuilding of Paris to three men: Baron Georges Haussmann, an urbanist and financier; Jean Charles Alphand, a planner and landscape gardener; and, most importantly of all, Eugene Belgrand, a designer of sewers.

Haussmann imposed a rigorous plan on the city and its architecture. As his project proceeded to destroy sections of the city that had existed for centuries there were, of course, protests, but the government continued making compulsory purchases of vast tracts of land, clearing away centuries of the city's heritage.

With a foresight much appreciated today, the authorities employed photographers to record the disappearing capital, two of whom devoted years of their lives to recording the massive changes taking place in Paris: Eugène Atget and Charles Marville. Much of their work is illustrated in the pages of this book.

As these photos illustrate, the new city was one of long avenues and wide boulevards, which were lined with grand apartment buildings of uniform width, height, and style. The city more than doubled in size with the annexation of outlying villages in 1859. The population grew from 1,000,000 to 1,696,000, and the twenty administrative districts of today were created. Thousands were obliged to move out of the city, as suddenly they were subjected to Paris taxes that they could not pay. They were soon replaced by a new population of wealthy bankers and industrialists, eager to move into the beautiful new capital.

Two principal aspects governed the rebuilding of Paris: national security and health and hygiene. The plan for improving national security was based upon the introduction of the wide avenues that replaced the narrow streets that in early days revolutionary Parisians could easily barricade when fighting their government. The avenues were equally suitable for maneuvering armies and transporting artillery. Improving health and hygiene in the city involved opening up and airing the once narrow, polluted streets, the building of social housing, schools, hospitals, and, of course, the famous sewers.

Although the reign of Napoleon III was undoubtedly the catalyst for making the city what it is today, the story of Paris is one that covers more than 2,000 years, and remarkably, the city has safeguarded wonderful evidence of its heritage from every age. The origins of the city can be traced from prehistoric times to the present by simply walking through the streets. The Latin Quarter still uses part of its Gallo-Roman street plan, and ruins of both Roman arenas and baths can be seen. There are traces of Merovingian and Carolingian history, and many fragments of the medieval city have survived. There is nothing more exciting or pleasurable to do in the city than seek fragments of the past, now woven into the fabric of today; this is what the following pages aim to do.

The Arc de Triomphe is as much a symbol of Paris as the Eiffel Tower. Built for Napoleon Bonaparte, like the triumphal arches of the ancient Roman Empire, it symbolized his capturing of the capital. Although embellished with sculptures and inscriptions to glorify the empire and the emperor, it was never completed during his lifetime. In 1840, some eighteen years after his death on the island of St. Helena, his funeral cortège passed through the arch, which had finally been completed.

The monumental sculptures crowning the arch were never cast in bronze and were eventually removed. The arch is now surrounded by one hundred posts linked by chains. These symbolize the return of the emperor Napoleon for one hundred days after his notorious escape from Elba. The body of an unknown soldier from World War I has been buried here since November 11, 1920. The eternal flame of remembrance that burns beneath the arch was first lit on Armistice Day 1923. Now open to the public, spectacular views across the city can be enjoyed from the rooftop terrace.

The Champs Elysées area was completely landscaped to create a vast open-air theater in which Napoleon hoped that parades to celebrate his military victories would take place. The gentle slope that rises from Place de la Concorde to Place de l'Etoile forms the stage, while the arch itself would be the theater's backdrop. In this picture a parade is taking place in honor of Edward VII, who was a frequent visitor to Paris at the end of the nineteenth century. The original equestrian statues at the entrance to the avenue, now replaced by copies, are in the Louvre. They once decorated the horses' drinking trough at the royal palace of Marly.

Today the Champs Elysées is still associated with prestige and glamour. In this view, seen from the famous Tuileries Gardens, the Arc de Triomphe can be seen in the distance, just behind the ancient obelisk. The avenue has become one of the most glamorous shopping areas in Europe. It is still used for hosting the city's festivities, including the famous military parade on Bastille Day. The Tour de France bicycle race ends on the celebrated avenue every July, and there are regular exhibitions of modern sculpture that have attracted crowds.

This was once a royal square laid out between 1755 and 1775 and named after Louis XV. It is octagonal in shape. In 1792 the square was renamed Place de la Révolution. It was here that the guillotine stood and Louis XVI and Marie Antoinette were beheaded in 1793. The name Concorde was chosen later, signaling the hope of a return to peace and normality. The obelisk in the center of the square, which was deemed an appropriate replacement for the statue of the king, is 3,300 years old and carved with hieroglyphics. This photograph, probably taken shortly before World War I, illustrates the blend of early motorized traffic with the few remaining horses and buggies.

Today the view is little changed, with imposing buildings on either side of the obelisk. The pavilion to the left, originally four private mansions, is now the renowned Hôtel Crillon and home of the prestigious l'Automobile-Club de France (the Automobile Club of France). The pavilion to the right, originally the furniture store for the royal palaces, is now the headquarters of the French Navy. The American Embassy is to the far left, and in the distance in the center is the Madeleine Church. The central obelisk has been restored and its tip reguilded, as it would have been in ancient Egypt.

In each corner of the Place de la Concorde, a statue symbolizes a French town. This view of the personification of Strasbourg in 1871 shows the figure covered in wreathes and other symbols lamenting France's loss of this town, the capital of Alsace. After the Franco-Prussian War and the Siege of Paris by the Prussians, a peace treaty was signed by which the French government relinquished Alsace and Lorraine. This aroused the fury of the French citizens, leading to an uprising against the government in a movement known as "the Commune."

The plinth of the statue dates back to the eighteenth century and is one of eight designed by Jacques Gabriel, the architect responsible for the square. The plinths gave access to sunken gardens but remained empty until the reign of Louis-Philippe, "the Citizen King," who ordered the statues and fountains. The statue itself, an allegory of the city of Strasbourg, was sculpted in the nineteenth century by the Swiss sculptor James Pradier. He used as his model the beautiful actress Juliette Drouet, later the mistress and muse of Victor Hugo.

France fell in June 1940, and the government fled to Bordeaux. Parisians left the capital in exile, joining six million refugees on the roads of France. On June 14, the Germans entered Paris. Marshal Pétain sued for peace, and the Third Republic ended, replaced by an "Etat Français," with its headquarters at Vichy and subject to the Germans. The occupation lasted for four years. In June 1944, the allies landed in Normandy, beginning the liberation of France. General Dietrich von Choltitz, who disobeyed Hitler's orders to destroy the city, surrendered to General Jacque-Philippe Leclerc on August 25, 1944, and Charles de Gaulle entered Paris that afternoon.

Today the square bears no real reminder of the toll of four years of occupation. The building in front of which the fighting took place is the seat of the French Navy. This area of town was the main headquarters of occupied Paris, which was administered from the Hôtel Crillon, the other pavilion on the square. The area is still renowned for its restaurants, such as Maxim's, and luxury shops where German soldiers bought silk stockings, perfume, cosmetics, and clothing to send home to their families.

This photograph was taken around 1860 from the central courtyard of the Louvre, looking west toward the palace gardens and the Champs Elysées. The Queen's Garden can be seen in the foreground. The wing of the building, which here obscures the view of the gardens, is the Tuileries Palace, which was built as a widow's palace by Queen Catherine de Medici after the untimely death of her husband, Henry II. It was from this palace that Louis XVI and Marie Antoinette escaped to Varennes shortly before their imprisonment during the Revolution.

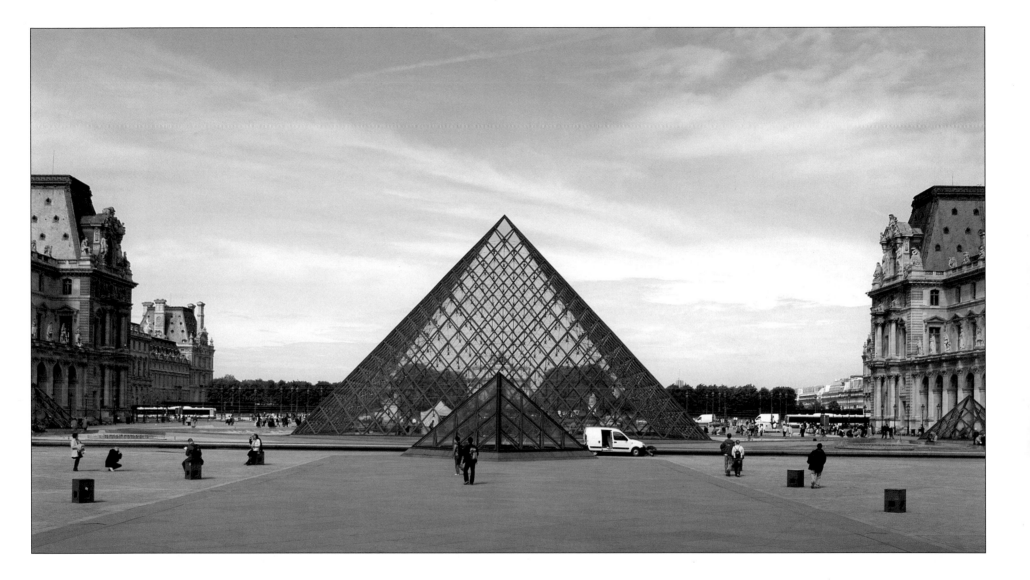

Today the view is greatly changed. The vista has been opened up by the destruction of the Tuileries Palace during the Commune in 1871. The scene is now dominated by I. M. Pei's glass pyramids, which now make up the new main entrance to the Louvre. The new complex was inaugurated in 1989 to celebrate the bicentennial of the Revolution. The renovated Richelieu wing, seen here on the right, was opened in 1994 to celebrate the 200th anniversary of the Louvre opening as a museum.

The façade of the church was photographed in 1852, the first year of Haussmann's great urban project. The church is situated opposite the colonnade of the Louvre, and when the Valois court moved into the palace, it became the royal church of Paris and was bestowed with gifts. On August 25, 1572, the bells ringing from the church were the signal for the terrible St. Bartholomew massacre. On this occasion hundreds of Huguenots (Protestants), gathered for the wedding of the Protestant Henry of Navarre to Princess Margot, were slaughtered by French soldiers.

Today the church still stands, thanks to Haussmann. A new avenue, named after Queen Victoria, was to be built from the Hôtel de Ville up to the façade of the Louvre. Haussmann cut the avenue short, saving the church from destruction. As a Protestant himself, he did not want to be accused of destroying a monument to those who had perished in the massacres. The church was the burial place of many famous artists and architects who were given lodgings in the Louvre once the king moved his court to Versailles. Today painters come here on the first Sunday of Lent for a special service to pray for fellow artists who have died during the year.

This lovely square is a superb example of the regal grace of architecture in France during the seventeenth century. This was a royal square originally designed by Jules Hardouin Mansart as a setting for a statue of Louis XIV. Its name comes from a residence that existed here previously, the home of the Duke of Vendôme, an illegitimate son of King Henry IV. The central column was ordered by Napoleon. Cast from some 2,000 cannons captured at the battle of Austerlitz, it was inspired by Emperor Trajan's Column in Rome. Napoleon had envisaged being buried in its base. It was pulled down during the Commune in 1871 (see above).

Today the column once again graces the center of the square. The 132-foot bronze column, originally built around a stone core, was reerected after the Commune. Seven different statues succeeded each other on the top of the column. Each different regime required a different statue! The present figure is a replica of the original, put back during the Third Republic. Today Place Vendôme is renowned worldwide for its jewelry stores—Van Cleef & Arpels, Boucheron, Chaumet—and for its banks. The square is also the location of the Ritz hotel, from which Princess Diana made her last, fateful journey.

The Paris Opera was the focal point of Haussmann's new Paris, located at the junction of the city's elegant new boulevards. The little-known architect Charles Garnier was chosen out of 171 contestants, but the project was slow to be finished due to the discovery of water underground that could not be drained away. This gave rise to the story of the famous "phantom of the opera," although the water is not a natural lake and the tale was imagined by the novelist Gaston Leroux. The water came from the original course of the river Seine, which once had a deeper meander before retreating to its present position. The house was opened in 1875, but the authorities "forgot" to invite the architect. They claimed it was an oversight, but it was more likely a show of their displeasure at his going over his budget. Garnier was obliged to buy his own ticket, but the public gave him an ovation.

Garnier's design was elaborate and colorful, with marble, mosaics, and gilding, and the building has been recently restored to its original splendor. A statue of Apollo, the god of the arts and music, crowns the top of the building, holding a golden lyre. The architect had wanted the building surrounded by gardens and waterfalls, but in fact it now presides over one of the busiest city squares.

Since the construction of the new opera house in Bastille Square in 1989, this building is mainly used for ballet productions, as the nineteenth-century design does not allow for the storage of much scenery. In the sumptuously upholstered red and gold auditorium, which seats some 2,000 people, is the famous ceiling painted by Chagall in 1964.

By decree of Napoleon, this building was to be a "Temple to the Glory of the Great Army." Like the Arc de Triomphe, it wasn't completed during his reign. The church went through many vicissitudes, narrowly escaping becoming Paris's first railway station in 1837. It was eventually completed and consecrated in 1842. The design of the church is inspired by a Greek temple, with a peristyle and no lateral windows. The interior is lit by skylights. It is surrounded by fifty-two majestic Corinthian columns, each one sixty-two feet tall. The position of organist at this church has always been a coveted one, and both Gabrile Fauré and Camille Saint-Saëns held the post for many years. The funeral of Chopin, who died nearby on Place Vendôme, was held here in 1849.

The church has recently been cleaned, which highlights the huge pediment sculptures. The scene shows the Last Judgment. Christ stands in the center, with the elect to his right and the damned to his left, being chased away by an angel. Mary Magdalene, to whom the church is dedicated, intercedes on behalf of the damned. She symbolizes the importance of repentance. With its magnificent approach and monumental stairway of twenty-eight steps, this church used to be a favorite for society weddings. The square is now famed for its pretty flower market and fabulous food stores, including Fauchon, Hediard, Caviar Kaspia, and Marquise de Sévigné chocolates.

The buildings on the boulevard des Capucines are typical of the new and elegant architecture that replaced the filthy, narrow, winding streets of "old Paris." At this time the façade of the building became the outward and visible sign of the social status of those that lived within. The balcony on the second floor that runs the length of the boulevard signifies the most prestigious floor. As the building gets higher, the prestige and the decorative schemes diminish. The buildings at this time were limited to six stories; the last floor housed the servants' rooms and the ground floor was used for retail.

The boulevard owes its name to the Convent of Capucines (nuns adhering to the Franciscan order) that was here until the Revolution. It is one of six that radiate from prestigious Place de l'Opera. Little changed, the ground floors consist of rows of fashionable stores and restaurants. Today the sidewalks are still lined with kiosks and stalls. Many of the lovely apartments have become offices, as there are few Parisians who can afford the luxury of living here. Jacques Offenbach, the father of the cancan, lived and died in the first house on the left.

This photo shows the famous Parisian store around 1900. It is said that the department store was born in Paris! At the turn of the century new buses allowed people to travel easily across the city to do their shopping, which led to the creation of establishments such as the Galeries Lafayette. The architectural revolution of the nineteenth century had brought new techniques and materials necessary for these immense shopping palaces.

Builders, inspired by the cathedrals of the past, designed flying buttresses, now in steel, and covered them with vast expanses of the newly developed plate glass that could also be used for huge store windows for fashionable displays. The decorated interior of Galeries Lafayette, with its grand staircase and stained glass dome, was in the style of the newly built opera house.

Boulevard Haussmann is still a major shopping street and both the Galeries Lafayette and Printemps, the two famous stores that date back to the late nineteenth century, survive. Today the sidewalks still throng with shoppers and tourists, and stalls abound selling everything imaginable, encouraging shoppers to come through the doors. Inside the Galeries Lafayette, the grand staircase has been dismantled, but otherwise the decorative interior can still be admired. Every Christmas thousands of families come to admire the animated window displays where toys magically come to life to entertain the crowds of children, who stand on specially designed ramps to allow them to see in. The Christmas lights are always a spectacular show.

The rue du Fauborg St. Denis is one of the most ancient streets in Paris, leading north to the church of St. Denis, where the kings were buried. The word *faubourg*, "suburb," indicates that this part of the street was once outside the city walls. This view is captured from the fauborg, looking toward the center of the city. In the distance can be seen the St. Denis arch. This gate, designed by architect François Blondel, was built in 1672 for Louis XIV on the site of a medieval gateway that the Sun King had just had demolished. The arch celebrates the victories of the French army in the Rhineland as they pushed the border of France eastward. In the nineteenth century this was still a busy thoroughfare with carts making their way into Paris.

Today the rue du Faubourg St. Denis is still an extremely busy road leading from the station serving the east of France, the Gare de l'Est, to the center of the city. The horse-drawn wagons have been replaced by vans and cars, but the area is still a lively market quarter. It is now the center of the "rag trade" in Paris, home to the fashion wholesalers. The immigrant workers employed here have inspired stores and restaurants with their countries' specialties.

This station serves the northwest suburbs and Normandy. The original train line was built in 1832 and ran to St. Germain-en-Lay. It was financed by the Rothschilds to enable their guests and friends to visit them easily. Between 1886 and 1889 the station was rebuilt, growing from the Place de l'Europe to the rue de Rome, as can be seen here. The nineteenth-century French painters wanted to record the modern world. Monet, who took trains from this station regularly to reach his house at Argentueil, and later Giverny, was fascinated by the modern technology and painted many views of the trains amid clouds of steam as they arrived in the station.

Today an estimated 150 million people use the station every year, coming in to Paris from the western suburbs and Normandy. The station now links directly with the Métro and the high-speed suburban railway, the RER. In a few minutes one can travel across Paris. This station was the main link on the route between Paris and London in the days when Charles Dickens used to visit, researching his book A *Tale of Two Cities*. This service has now been replaced by the Channel Tunnel trains that depart from the Gare du Nord. The station façade was rebuilt for the Universal Exposition of 1900, and the elegant station hotel, the Concorde St. Lazare, was and still is intended for the many travelers who flock to the attractions of the city.

The Gare du Nord was built in 1863 by Jacques-Ignace Hittorf, who had designed the layout of Place de la Concorde and Place de l'Etoile. His works were little appreciated by Baron Haussmann, who directed the city planning, and it was probably this that led Haussmann to refuse the building of a grand avenue leading up to the station. The façade is decorated with colossal allegorical figures who symbolize towns in northern France and Europe served by the station. Rail travel revolutionized life in the nineteenth century, making journeys quick and comfortable and allowing working people to escape from Paris on their Sundays off to enjoy themselves in the forests, country villages, and riverside inns.

Today the station is international, with the famous sleek French high-speed trains arriving from Brussels, Amsterdam, and London. Hittorf's graceful design, with glass roofs supported by slender iron columns, was so efficient that the station has been able to absorb the ever-increasing traffic with few modifications. However, an ultramodern glass hall and shopping center has recently been added that enables a liaison between the suburban trains, the Métro, a new station link, and the Eurostar high-speed trains to London.

Built in the mid-nineteenth century, the Gare de l'Est station, with its semicircular rose window and crowned by a statue representing the town of Strasbourg, serves the eastern suburbs of Paris and the eastern provinces of Alsace and Lorraine. For this reason the local area has always been renowned for its markets selling specialties from the east of France and brasseries where beer and sauerkraut are served. Queen Victoria arrived here in 1855 when she came to Paris for the first Universal Exhibition. Napoleon III welcomed her and named an avenue after her—the avenue Victoria, beside the Hotel de Ville in central Paris. The queen commented in her diary, "The Emperor has done wonders for Paris."

The station was significantly enlarged in the late 1920s and early 1930s and has two entrances that are interesting examples of the art deco style. It is still the station at which the Orient Express arrives. The station was doubled in size with a second identical pavilion that is crowned by a statue of the town of Verdun, where many soldiers perished during World War I. Wounded soldiers were transported from the front via this station to hospitals in Paris during the war. The area today is lively and residential, the old commercial warehouses between the railway tracks and the canal nearby have become trendsetting stores, and the old industrial area has been replaced by bars and loft-style apartments.

The original Châtelet was a massive medieval barbican that protected the bridge leading to the royal palace on the island. The castle survived until just after the Revolution, when it was used as a prison, and it was eventually demolished between 1802 and 1810, leaving room for the large new square. The two theaters were built by the architect Gabriel Davioud, who also designed the famous St. Michel fountain, in 1862. In its early days the Théâtre du Châtelet became famous for its show *Around the World in Eighty Days*, based on the story of the balloon journey by Jules Verne. The man who inspired this story was Nadar, one of the first French photographers who pioneered photography from a balloon.

Today the square marks the geographical center of Paris. The few horse-drawn carts of bygone days have been replaced with particularly heavy traffic. The Théâtre du Châtelet is now devoted to concerts and opera performances with international celebrities. The auditorium can seat 1,400 more people than the Opéra Garnier. The theater opposite, which is almost identical, was bought by Sarah Bernhardt in 1899, who, being slim and beautiful, famously played Hamlet and Napoleon's young son in the play *L'Aiglon*.

One of the important improvements to Paris organized by Napoleon in the early nineteenth century was the provision of fountains. These brought fresh water, which was desperately needed, to the people of the city. The fountain in this picture was built in 1808 and decorated to commemorate Napoleonic victories. It was called the "Palm Fountain" and designed in the Egyptian style made popular during his reign, after his campaigns in Egypt. The figure on the column represents fame and glory with her two laurel-wreath crowns. She is also appropriate as a symbol of the dreams of the actors in the theaters here, as well as the military victories.

The fountain was moved in the mid-nineteenth century to its present-day position. When the boulevard de Sebastopol was built, the column was transported just forty feet to the west of its old location. This was a feat of engineering at the time; a special rail track was created and the entire monument, some twenty-four tons in weight and sixty-six feet high, was then wheeled on rails. It was reerected on a new base decorated with four sphinxes and allegories of Prudence, Fortitude, Truth, and Justice. These are the virtues a ruler should exercise, and sculptures representing these qualities were often found on monuments to kings.

The main city cemetery stood on this spot between the twelfth and eighteenth centuries. Parisians were buried in communal graves, their bodies covered with lime until the flesh had been eaten away. Once the bones were bare, they were stacked up in the rafters of the charnel house around the square. This practice ended just before the Revolution. The charnel houses were cleared and the bones were transferred to the ancient quarries, now called the Catacombs. The square subsequently became part of the main Paris fresh-produce market. This view of Place des Innocents was taken about 1852, just before the rebuilding of Paris, and shows the traders on the fringe of the Les Halles market.

The architecture of the square is little changed. The lovely Renaissance fountain is still in place and has been restored. The *innocents* who gave their name to the square were those massacred by Herod, as described in the Bible, but later on the Parisians ironically named the prostitutes that washed in the fountains the "innocents." Today the square and the area immediately around it is lined with trendy clothing stores and filled with skaters and skateboarders.

The famous fresh-produce market was located here for nearly eight hundred years. The name comes from food halls built here around 1200. In the nineteenth century the market was redesigned under great halls of glass and steel. This central market fed all of Paris, selling to the hotel and restaurant trade as well as supplying local markets. The French author Émile Zola wrote a novel about it, calling it the "belly of Paris." By 1969, the congestion caused by deliveries, trucks, porters, and mountains of produce led to its closure.

Inset: The porters of Les Halles were a vital part of the machinery of the market. They were renowned for their humor and their market cries. Here they can be seen wearing their traditional sombrero-like hats, which protected their necks from the heavy loads they carried.

To the dismay and outcry of Parisians, the old halls were demolished in the 1970s. The new development consists of a huge underground shopping mall, with new gardens at ground level. These have been decorated with metallic structures by the artists Claude and François-Xavier Lalanne, designed to evoke the original architecture. The wholesalers to the catering trade can still be found here; chefs come from all over the world to buy cooking equipment and "front of house" items from stores such as Dehillerin and Simon. In the old days people came here late at night to eat the onion soup, a local specialty, because it was cheap and fortifying. This traditional dish can still be enjoyed here today.

The rue St. Bon is a charming little backstreet in the Châtelet area. This photograph was taken around 1906 and is a good example of the type of narrow cobbled street that Baron Haussmann was clearing to replace with his wide avenues and boulevards. The building visible in the distance is the Gothic church of St. Médéric; the church tower houses Paris's oldest bell, made in 1331. The walls of the street are covered with posters advertising a variety of goods from Singer sewing machines and *gentiane suze* (still a popular aperitif drink today) to a concert performance by a child star, "La Môme Phémie." Child stars were very popular at this time and it would not be long before *la môme* Piaf would take the country by storm.

Today the rue St. Bon is a picturesque, but quiet street that cuts from the busy rue de Rivoli to the ancient rue de la Verrerie. The view has hardly changed, although the façades of the buildings have been cleaned and restored. The advertisements have long disappeared, as has the sign of the cross keys, that advertised a locksmith. The street owes its name to a chapel dedicated to St. Bon, built in 1125 but destroyed by revolutionaries. Today the church of St. Médéric is affectionately known as "St. Merry," and its ancient bell, the oldest in Paris, as "La Merry."

This wonderful photograph shows the old grain market of Paris being demolished before being rebuilt in 1899. In the background is the lovely Renaissance church of St. Eustache. On the right is the astrology tower that was built for the superstitious queen Marie de Medici. It was from here that her fortune-teller Ruggieri is said to have predicted her death. The origin of the word "disaster" is *des astres*, or "from the stars." This is an excellent illustration of the old belief in the power of the stars to influence our daily lives.

The old grain market was made obsolete by the advent of the railways to transport grain and the building of large silos to stock it before distribution. The building was rebuilt in 1899 as a commodities exchange, where professional bodies fixed trading conditions for grain, sugar, oils, and alcohol. The building was bought by the Paris Chamber of Commerce after World War II. Markets are still negotiated here for coffee, cocoa, and white sugar. The building was recently restored and has a fine painted ceiling showing trade from all corners of the world.

The Samaritaine department store, which stands on the banks of the Seine at Pont Neuf, takes its name from the old Samaritaine water pump, which once supplied water to the Parisians. The buildings are perfect examples of industrial architecture between 1900 and 1930. The domed building at the rear was built by Frantz Jourdain. It uses riveted steel, with great window bays and mosaic decorations. The riverfront buildings in the foreground of the photo were demolished in 1926, and Henri Sauvage and Jourdain replaced them with what is now one of the best examples of art deco in Paris.

Today the Samaritaine is still one of the most popular department stores in Paris. It is an excellent example of how late-nineteenth-century industrialists could make a fortune out of hard work and diligence. The founder, Ernest Cognacq, started as a small storekeeper, and with his wife, Louise Jay, built up a vast department store. The pair were great patrons of the arts and collected eighteenth-century art and furniture, which they bequeathed to the city of Paris. (The Musée Cognacq-Jay in the Marais district.) The public has access to the rooftop terrace of the store, which offers spectacular views across the city.

540 PARIS. – Matelassières sur les quais. – LL.

The Pont Neuf (New Bridge) is ironically the oldest in Paris. The first stone was laid by Henry III in 1578, but the bridge was inaugurated by Henry IV. It had taken nearly thirty years to build. The quayside to the left, Quai des Grands Augustins, is the oldest in the city, built in 1313. Trades and crafts have been practiced along the riverside and under the bridges for centuries. Mattresses were both made and repaired here because the workers could take refuge under the bridge if it rained. Mattresses were coveted as prestigious possessions in the past and were even included in wills. One can still see the mattress-sterilizing machine in the Credit Municipale (the Paris Pawnbrokers Museum)!

Today one still marvels at the technical prowess of the sixteenth-century builders. This was the first bridge to have been built from stone rather than wood and the first to have open views across the river, as it was not lined with houses on either side. The bridge was made up of twelve arches decorated with humorously grotesque masks and had sidewalks, an innovation at the time. The bridge has been magnificently restored, the quayside much widened, and the craftsmen and artisans replaced with Parisian strollers.

The rue de Rivoli crosses the city east to west, linking the town hall, the Louvre, Place de la Concorde, and the Champs Elysées. It was built for Napoleon and named after his victory at Rivoli in Italy in 1797. This was a major urban development, being built above splendid new sewers. Napoleon had dreamed of rebuilding Paris, but as he was busy at war and reorganizing the administration of the empire, the project was to be carried out later under his nephew, Napoleon III. In the foreground to the left is the Hôtel de Ville and in the background to the right is the medieval Tour St. Jacques.

Today the rue de Rivoli is one of the busiest thoroughfares of the capital, visited for its elegant stores located under the lovely arcades designed by Charles Percier and Pierre-François Fontaine for the emperor. One of the most famous addresses today is number 266, Angelina's tearoom, celebrated for the Belle Époque interior décor and their fabulous Mont Blanc pastries. At number 288 is the Hotel Meurice, from which the German general Dietrich Von Choltitz refused to obey Hitler's order to blow up the bridges of Paris, enabling the city to be liberated intact.

On June 10, 1889, the tower opened its doors to the public. The first visitor was the Prince of Wales, later Edward VII. He and his family had come to Paris for the Universal Exhibition, for which the tower had been built. The project was begun on January 28, 1887, and completed some two years later in March 1889. It was named after its designer, the brilliant French engineer Gustave Eiffel. When it was built, it was the tallest tower in the world, standing at nearly 1,000 feet tall. Its closest competitor was the Washington Monument, 555 feet high, completed the year before. As the tower grew stage by stage, half of Paris marveled at the sight, while the other half was horrified. Three hundred artists and writers signed a protest against the tower; they did not want it to remain in place for the twenty years originally intended. In 1940, when Hitler was visiting Paris, the Resistance put the elevators out of order so that he could not go up. In 1944, at the liberation, firemen raced to the top to hoist a huge homemade French flag.

This view is from the top of the Chaillot hill. Today the panorama includes the Champ de Mars, originally the training ground for cadets at the military school, the elegant school building itself (visible in the distance behind the tower), and a stunning view of the tower. Visitors to the tower can walk up the 1,671 steps or take elevators, stopping at the first floor (189 feet), the second floor (379 feet), and then at the summit at 906 feet! The actual height of the tower can vary by as much as seven inches depending on the temperature. The maximum sway at the top due to wind can be as much as four and a half inches. The view from the top is said to be best just before sunset, at which time Chartres, fifty-five miles from Paris, can be seen.

The square was named Trocadero after the French military victory at Trocadero, in the Bay of Cadiz, which had been reenacted on the hill here. Napoleon ordered the plateau of the Chaillot hill to be flattened with the idea of building a splendid palace here for his son, the king of Rome. The palace was never built. The building in the photo was designed by the architects Davioud and Bardet in the Moorish style as a central feature of the Universal Exhibition of 1878. Critics said it looked like a donkey wearing a straw beach hat with ear holes. It survived as an example of the architecture of its era until 1937, when it was replaced by the Chaillot Palace.

The Chaillot Palace was built as a pavilion for the last Universal Exhibition held in Paris, in 1937. The rather severe and sober rigor of its portico and façades heralded a new age in architecture and design. During the world's fair in 1937, just before the war, both the Russian and German pavilions stood glowering at each other just in front of this building. Today the palace houses the Musée de la Marine (Maritime Museum), the Musée de l'homme (Museum of Anthropology), the Musée des Monuments Français (Museum of French Monuments), and a large theater, the Théâtre Nationale de Chaillot.

103. — Maximum de la crue au Pont de l'Alma. — C M

This picture was taken during the terrible floods of 1910. Crowds of people have gathered on the Left Bank to watch the river, which seems about to burst its banks. This bridge was built just before 1855 to commemorate Napoleon III's victory in the Crimea and to improve access to the city's first Universal Exhibition. The original bridge was decorated with four sculpted military figures, three of which, including *le chasseur* (the hunter), visible here, were removed when the bridge was rebuilt.

By the 1960s the bridge had actually sunk nearly three feet into the bed of the Seine. A new bridge had to be constructed, and rebuilding began in the early 1970s. The present bridge is made up of two arches that span the river, resting on just one bridge pile. The concrete foundations of the bridge have been sunk 120 feet beneath the surface of the river. Out of the four original statues only the much-loved Zouave found a home on the new bridge. He is considered the marker of high water.

This image is an evocative reminder of the old villages that surrounded Paris until they became part of the city in 1860. What is now the sixteenth of the twenty districts that make up Paris was three villages: Passy, Chaillot, and Auteuil, where there were fields, orchards, and vineyards. The white house on the right was the home of the novelist Honoré de Balzac in the 1840s. He wrote a number of novels and stories with reappearing characters. One of his main themes was that greed or self-interest always triumphs over love.

Today the scene has hardly changed and the village atmosphere still pervades. The street has been recobbled but still has its old protective posts along the right-hand side. Balzac's home is now a museum dedicated to his life and work. It is said that the writer, who had a talent for unlucky investment, chose to live here because he could easily escape from his creditors. The house is hidden from view from the road, and the back door visible in the photo provided a suitable secret exit by which he could flee undetected. Balzac's works show the influence of his money problems. Today a guard stands watch over the entrance to the Turkish ambassador's residence, which is behind the walls on the left.

André Citroën, who lived from 1878 to 1935, was a brilliant industrialist and engineer. He started as an arms manufacturer, and in 1915 he opened his first factory, near the Eiffel Tower. It was capable of making 55,000 explosive shells a day. After the war he undertook the serial manufacture of motorized vehicles, the first of which was ready in 1919. He soon had factories in St. Ouen, Clichy, and Levallois and became one of the inventors of production-line manufacturing. In 1934 he produced the celebrated front-wheel drive model, the Traction. No French gangster film remake is complete without one of these. The much-loved 2CV came out in 1948.

Today the crashing and whirring of heavy industry has been replaced with the calm of an avant-garde park. The only sound is of fountains and water jets. In the early 1990s, two famous landscape gardeners, Gilles Clément and Alain Provost, collaborated to create a garden of the senses, encompassing four themes: artifice, architecture, movement, and nature.

The elegant façade of Notre Dame is one of the symbols of Paris. The church was built in the twelfth and thirteenth centuries and expresses the prosperity of medieval Paris. Its beautiful rose window still has its original thirteenth-century glass. Two massive towers house the famous bells. The cathedral was neglected in the eighteenth century and nearly destroyed during the Revolution. It had not yet been restored when this picture was taken; its spire is missing, as are the statues in the gallery above the entrance portals. Victor Hugo's famous novel about Quasimodo, the hunchbacked bell ringer, published in 1831, incited the Parisians to call for the cathedral to be restored.

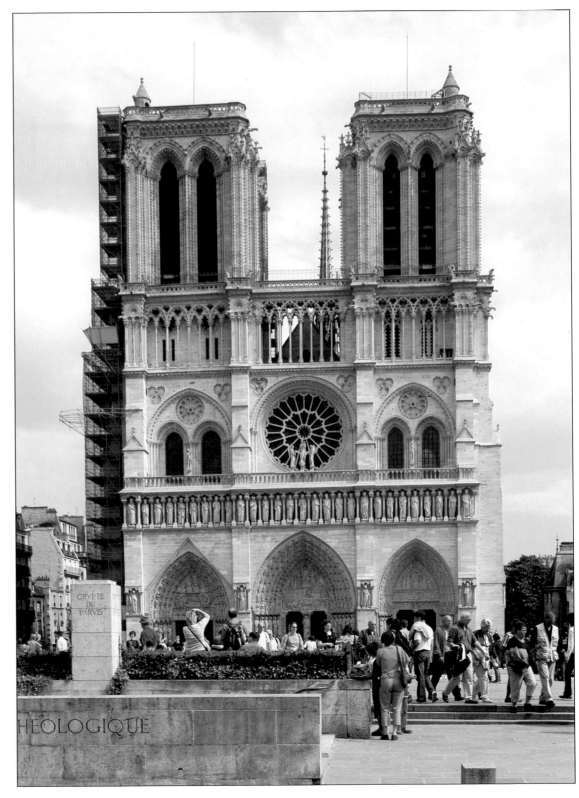

Today the whole area is much changed, with the buildings in front of the cathedral demolished to create a large square. The façade has been completely cleaned and restored, and statues of the biblical kings now stand in the gallery. The architect Eugene Viollet-le-Duc and a team of stonemasons lovingly restored the church to its former glory. The original spire had been struck by lightning but a remarkable new one, using modern materials, replaced it. The façade and towers are open to the public as a museum. A spectacular view of both the architecture of the church and the panorama of Paris can be enjoyed from the top of the towers.

This ancient Left Bank street, with its patchwork of architectural styles, affords a view of the flying buttresses of the cathedral. This incredible architectural feature is a testimony to the prowess of the medieval builders. The beautiful light buttresses enabled the churches to rise much higher than before by supporting the weight of the roof. Thus the walls could be pierced with large windows, which would then be filled with beautiful stained glass, flooding the church with colored light.

Today the view is little changed. The small chapel with the pointed roof beside the cathedral is the treasury where the Crown of Thorns is kept. It is put on display once a year on Good Friday. This quarter, called Maubert after a medieval teacher, is now a quiet backstreet of delightful residences in tastefully converted ancient buildings. The little streets of this village still bear their evocative names of the past, one of which is rue des Rats—"Rat Street"! In medieval times this area was the heart of the student community, and all lessons were conducted in Latin. It is for this reason that this area is called Le Quartier Latin (the Latin Quarter). Students continue to study here today.

The Hôtel de Ville started as a building for the chief merchant of Paris, located here because it dominated the principal shipping port and trading market of the city. The Seine is deep and wide at this point, so boat traffic could dock and unload goods for trading. This view shows the Hôtel de Ville in ruins. In 1871, after the end of the Franco-Prussian War, the revolutionary Commune took control of the city. The Commune lasted for two months and when the government forces entered Paris in May of that year, the Federalists set fire to both the Town Hall Building and the Tuileries Palace before the Commune was crushed. Here the building is seen as a burned-out ruin.

Today the building houses the offices of the mayor of Paris and is Paris's official reception building. It was completely rebuilt after the fire of 1871 and its façades are now decorated with 146 statues of illustrious Parisians. On the roof stand guardsmen who symbolize the twenty-two regions of France. The square in front, once the medieval market and place of execution where Esmeralda was burned at the stake in *The Hunchback of Notre Dame*, is now a showcase for the city. There are many annual festivals here, including La Fete du Pain (the Bread Festival), and every Christmas it becomes an open-air ice-skating rink.

The western end of the Île de la Cité has been the location of a palace since ancient times. The parts of the building visible in the photograph are the royal chapel, the law courts, and the prison. The medieval building fronting the river, with its four mighty towers, was the main royal palace in Paris until the kings moved to the Louvre in the fourteenth century. The hall, with its rounded windows, is the room where people pace up and down, waiting for their trials. It is referred to as *la salle des pas perdus* (the room of wasted steps).

The name of the building, the Conciergerie, comes from the title of the governor of the building, the concierge. It became famous during the Revolution as a prison where people were kept before their trials. Now a museum, the visitor can see the cell where Marie Antoinette was imprisoned before her execution, and a blade from the guillotine accompanies other memorabilia from this grim period of French history. In the previous photograph, the surrounding buildings had been cleared away before the construction of the new Tribunal de Commerce (the commercial law courts), which now obscure much of the view of the former palace.

The history of the Paris riverside booksellers goes back to the building of the Pont Neuf in the seventeenth century, when booksellers carried or pushed their stalls. The stands seen here date from the time of Napoleon III, who created them as a way for veterans of his army to earn a living. It was from his reign onward that the booksellers were allowed to leave their stalls permanently on the parapet of the river walls. Like the flea market, the *bouquinistes*, secondhand booksellers, were a favorite haunt of the surrealists, who took inspiration from this incongruous blend of objects and texts.

Today booksellers can be found on both the Left and Right Bank, from the Île Saint-Louis to the Louvre. There is no order to this market, like the flea market of Clignancourt; dealers mix together selling antique manuscripts, ancient maps, movie posters, and souvenirs of Paris. Nowadays each bookseller is allowed a maximum of about twenty-six feet of parapet space, his stall must be painted the standard green color, and his concession has to be renewed annually at the town hall. Some sites are well frequented, while other sellers complain of being "in purgatory."

There has been a bird market in Paris since medieval times. This lively photo of the market on the Île de la Cité, taken toward the end of the nineteenth century, captures its spirit. Two men on the left appear to be haggling over the price of canaries, and the vendor is clearly defending the quality of her merchandise. The bemused onlooker to the right is wearing the type of hat made famous by Toulouse Lautrec, while the little girl poses proudly with her new cage.

Cockatiels, canaries, and cages line the pavements of the market. Every Sunday the normal daily flower market on the Île de la Cité is replaced by the bird market. In the city, where people tend to live in small apartments, birds make popular pets. The market is always crowded with both adults and children. Nowadays the bird breeders have to be licensed members of the Ornithological Society, and the birds that they sell should be ringed and accompanied with a breeder's certificate. There are also stalls selling rabbits, guinea pigs, ferrets, and every other imaginable kind of small pet.

This extraordinary photograph was taken from the Petit Pont looking toward the Pont St. Michel on January 3, 1880. The city had been brought to a standstill by a winter so cold that the Seine had frozen. A spilled cargo of wine barrels is imprisoned in the ice. The painter Monet, living just outside Paris at Vetheuil but beside the river Seine, captured many scenes of this spectacular freeze on canvas. When the ice finally started to thaw and crack, he described the noise as similar to cannons being fired.

Today the quayside has been built up and widened to form a riverside promenade, but otherwise, the view is little changed. The Ns on the Pont St. Michel are the monogram of Napoleon III, during whose reign the bridge was rebuilt. This view shows the Seine between the island and the Left Bank, the narrow side of the river. This stretch was not opened to navigation until 1850. Today it is the realm of pleasure cruisers and the *bateaux-mouches* (riverboats), which head toward Notre Dame to dawdle in the shadows of the cathedral.

This view was taken from the Pont Louis Philippe, looking eastward against the flow of the Seine. On the left is the Right Bank; on the right is the Île Saint-Louis. When the photo was taken, this area was scruffy and run-down. The floating laundries were the realm of the washerwomen, as few people had running water in their homes. Bohemian painters, such as Degas, would come to study the women at work. The large floating structure in the foreground is a bathing pool, a necessary feature of old Paris as so many apartments were equipped with primitive washing facilities.

Once again the Île Saint-Louis is a chic residential quarter, as it was when it was first built in the seventeenth century. The floating laundries and other boat moorings have long since disappeared. The name of the bridge comes from the engineer who built it in the seventeenth century, Christophe Marie. Like other bridges in Paris it was originally built up with fifty houses. During the floods of March 1658, the two arches on the island side collapsed, along with twenty houses. The catastrophe caused sixty deaths. A temporary wooden bridge covered the gap and users had to pay a toll until enough money had been raised to finance the rebuilding.

The road is named after one of the chief merchants of Paris, Jean Juvenal des Ursins, who had a palace on this street in late medieval times. There is a magnificent portrait of him in the Louvre by the painter Jean Fouquet. This was one of a labyrinth of narrow winding streets that formed a little quarter beside Notre Dame. Originally this enclave had been the cloister and school buildings of the cathedral, but the school declined in importance once the university developed on the Left Bank in the thirteenth century.

Today the road is extremely pretty, quiet, and in a very desirable location. The old Hôtel des 2 Lions, photographed in 1923, was demolished and rebuilt in 1958 by a French architect named Fernand Pouillon. Pouillon has created a picturesque mock-medieval palace using elements of old buildings such as ironwork, window surrounds, and medieval doors. This twentieth-century folly, with magnificent views across the Seine, was lived in for a year by the architect before being occupied by the Aga Khan.

This lovely ancient street takes its name from a river that joined the Seine nearby. The river was used by the artisans of medieval Paris as a source of power for their mills and machinery. It also served as an open-air sewer. Because of this, the river was vaulted over in the nineteenth century. It still runs underground through Paris today and is twenty miles long. It is believed Dante lived in this street in the 1290s while beginning his great poem *The Divine Comedy*.

Today the architecture of this medieval street is little changed. This road had, however, become one of the last slum enclaves in central Paris and was due for demolition until President Mitterrand bought a substantial property here and renovated it. The street links the lovely market square of Place Maubert with the banks of the Seine, wending past little gardens, courtyards, and the façades of beautifully restored ancient houses.

This street cuts east-west through the center of Île de la Cité, ending opposite the entrance to the Palais de Justice, the law courts of Paris. This early nineteenth-century street is far removed from the medieval slums that Haussmann was clearing, as can be seen from the photograph. It was nevertheless demolished during the huge clearance taking place on the island. The east end of the street was lost to the building of the new charity hospital Hôtel Dieu, and the western end became a large open square. It is hard to imagine, standing on the open square today, the densely built-up island of the past.

Today the square is known as the rue de Lutèce, which was the name given to Paris in Roman times. The view of the façade of the law courts has been opened up, and it is here, to the right, that the flower and bird markets take place. The large complex of buildings to the left is the new Préfecture de Police (Police Headquarters) to which Parisians come for mundane tasks such as collecting identity cards and driving licenses. The building to the right is the Tribunal de Commerce (the Commercial Law Courts), crowned with a majestic dome.

The palace was built as a residence for Queen Marie de Medici after the death of her husband, Henry IV, in 1610. The architect Salomon de Brosse designed a residence inspired by the queen's childhood home in Florence, the Pitti Palace. The entrance pavilion seen here, with its cupola and rusticated columns, is decidedly Italian in influence. The palace was much admired, and in the 1620s Rubens was commissioned to paint a series of twenty-four paintings celebrating the reign of the queen to hang in the palace gallery. These pictures can now be seen in the Louvre.

Marie de Medici benefited little from the palace she had built. A plot she had organized backfired against her, and she was exiled by her son, Louis XIII. She ended her days in Cologne. During the Revolution, the palace became a prison. Camille Desmoulins, Fabre d'Eglantine, George-Jacques Danton, and the painter David were among those imprisoned here. Since the reign of Napoleon, the palace has been home to the Sénat, the upper house of the Paris parliament. The Sénat is composed of 238 members elected by both departmental and municipal councillors and deputies.

ah! Que ce temps est lointain où ,étant "petit", j'allais faire manœuvrer des flottes sur cette mer minuscule

155. - PARIS - Jardin du Luxembourg

The Luxembourg gardens are among the loveliest in Paris. Children and students have enjoyed these public gardens since the nineteenth century, and writers such as Victor Hugo have written lovingly about them. On this postcard the sender has written, "Oh how long ago, the days when as a child I would maneuver flotillas on this minuscule sea." The formal gardens, reflecting the rigor of the palace façade, are decorated with pretty flower beds, statues, and trees in massive white tubs that can be moved for protection into *orangeries*, or greenhouses, in the winter.

Sailing toy boats is still a popular activity today. In this much-loved garden, there are now tennis courts, pony rides, and a bandstand for open-air concerts. Performances at the puppet theater keep children and adults entranced throughout summer. Parisians make use of their public gardens because they mostly live in apartments. There are always crowds of children in the gardens, and the elderly play chess or *boules* (lawn bowling). There are beautifully kept orchards, looked after by the school of horticulture. The French National Society of Beekeepers has their hives here.

The Orsay railway station was built to solve the traffic problems that would be created by the huge influx of visitors to the Universal Exhibition of 1900. By 1938, the station, built too close to the city center, was closed down. The building illustrates the way the use of modern materials was blended with historical details at the time. The structure is steel but the coffered ceiling alludes to the Pantheon of ancient Rome. The great vault was designed to be able to accommodate clouds of steam, despite the fact that the trains were electrified by this time.

After the outcry caused by the destruction of the historic market halls, the city decided to restore rather than demolish this monumental station. In 1978 the decision was made to convert the station into a museum of nineteenth-century art. As can be seen in the photo, the structure of the building is little changed. The Italian architect Gae Aulenti has divided the vast space of the station into small galleries where the academic schools vie with paintings by impressionists, postimpressionists, and early modern painters.

Tucked away in the heart of the Latin Quarter is this charming enclave of old houses. In their heyday of the seventeenth century, they were among the most luxurious residences in the city. The little suite of courtyards, the Cour de Rohan, takes its name from the archbishops of Rouen in Normandy, who had their residence here. In these buildings, Diane de Poitiers, mistress of King Henry II, had an apartment. In the nineteenth century the painter Augustus John had a studio in these buildings, and the French composer Saint-Saëns was born here.

Today it is a marvelous surprise to turn off the noisy boulevard St. Germain and suddenly fall upon these three quiet, green leafy courtyards. Nowadays these are luxurious loft-style apartments, with large studio windows, balconies, terraces, and eccentric stairways and balustrades. These picturesque features were exploited when Collette's novella *Gigi* was filmed here in 1958. In the middle courtyard there is a curious iron tripod, a *pas de mule*, which was designed to assist a rider in mounting his horse or mule.

This road is named after one of the many famous Latin Quarter teachers associated with this area. Erasmus and Pierre Abelard also taught here. Erasmus, who lived here in the sixteenth century, referred to this little quarter as "that cesspit Maubert," an evocation of the noise, bustle, and mess of the narrow, cobbled medieval streets. The store to the right, marked "Enseignes," was that of a sign writer—examples of his work are displayed on the walls. In the past, every shop had a sign embellished with a picture as literacy was reserved for an elite. The stone posts to the right of the street were to protect the pedestrians from the perils of horse-drawn vehicles.

Running more or less parallel to the rue de Bièvre, this street was part of a slum area that narrowly escaped demolition. In both the mid-nineteenth century and later, after World War II, it was thought cheaper and more practical to demolish and rebuild from scratch than to restore historic architecture. When Mitterrand moved to the quarter, however, its future was changed. The houses along this road have been beautifully restored, there are now attractive restaurants and boutiques, and the façade of the sign-writers store has been preserved. A stroll along this road is like stepping back in time.

Medicine has been taught in this district since the fourteenth century. The learned scholars were physicians, while the "hands-on" doctors were the barber-surgeons, who specialized in bleeding. The doctors and surgeons had rival corporations until a new medical school (École de Médecine) was founded at the time of the Revolution. This street corner has many Revolutionary associations. In the foreground to the left were the ancient abbey buildings of the Cordeliers, which became the radical debating club that Camille Desmoulins and George-Jacques Danton belonged to. Jean-Paul Marat lived on this street when he was stabbed to death in his bathtub by Charlotte Corday.

The French poet Baudelaire was born on the street to the left. In his poem "The Swan," he lamented that "the shape of a city changes faster than a mortal's heart." Today the street is much changed indeed. The vast new medical school, built at the end of the nineteenth century, can be seen in the foreground on the right and left side of the street. The ancient building on the corner was completely restored in 1977 and has lost its elegant watchtower. It now houses a charming old-fashioned tearoom, the Patisserie Viennoise, a favorite among students for lunches or delicious pastries.

Originally a gateway into Paris in medieval times, by the eighteenth century this crossroads had become a central crossing point of the Left Bank. It was crowded with pedestrians, marketeers, and horse-drawn wagons. The St. Germain area developed as an aristocratic neighborhood when Louis XIV moved to Versailles and bridges were built across the Seine, making the Left Bank more accessible. In this photo we see the oysters displayed outside the café on the left, still a typical sight in Paris today, where seafood is much enjoyed. The store on the right rented suits, which would have been too expensive an item for most working people to have owned at the time.

Today the Buci crossroads is still a lively junction. A regular fresh produce market takes place nearby, attracting locals. The streets are lined with cafés, fine markets, flower shops, and restaurants. In fine weather the pavement tables are crowded with people enjoying the atmosphere. The square has been opened up and the traffic island has disappeared to make way for buses and cars. The façade of the café to the left is little changed and still has its pretty clock that keeps good time. The seafood stacked in baskets has made way for café tables. The *billards precision* (billiards) so popular in the nineteenth century and advertised on the façade have been replaced by slot machines.

This lovely old street, which climbs up the hill of St. Geneviève, wends its way to the ancient market street of rue Descartes, named after the philosopher Descartes. His way of thinking, referred to as "Cartesian," is still very much an aspect of the French approach to life. Descartes lived in the district in the seventeenth century. Around the time this photograph was taken, the disreputable poet Paul Verlaine, who had fallen on hard times, lived and died in poverty in the house set back from the street on the left. It is now a restaurant named after him. The first lines of his beautiful poem "Chanson d'Automne" ("Song of Autumn") were broadcast on BBC radio as a secret signal to inform the French that the D-Day landings in Normandy were about to begin.

Today the road is recognizably the same. The hoardings and advertisements painted on the sides of the houses have disappeared, the buildings have been cleaned up, and the old boutiques have been replaced with cheap and cheerful stores and restaurants. These cater to the many students from the nearby Sorbonne and other schools in the area. In the early 1920s, Ernest Hemingway lived nearby and rented a room in the house where Verlaine died. He later immortalized this district in his book *A Moveable Feast*. Many visitors now come on the trail of Hemingway, James Joyce, George Orwell, and other writers associated with the Latin Quarter.

This photo was taken in 1898. The square takes its name from the parish church on the right. St. Médard is the patron saint of umbrella makers, because it was said that if it rains on his day, it would rain for forty days! Climbing the hill to the left in the background is the famous rue Mouffetard fresh-produce market, crowded with shoppers and stalls. The name Mouffetard comes from an ancient French word, *la mouffe*, referring to the stink and squalor associated with the area because of the Bièvre River, which was used by all the dirty trades. The sculptor Rodin and the architect of the Paris Opera, Charles Garnier, were both born in relatively humble circumstances just off this street. Mouffetard traders are shown in the photo above.

As can be seen in the photo, the area is still a very popular market. This is primarily a residential area and local Parisians flock to choose from the wide variety of meat, fish, eggs, fruit, and choice vegetables. There are mouthwatering displays in the cheese shops and well-stocked wine merchants. Modern-day versions of the street vendors shown in the inset opposite can be seen here today, and French women still prefer the traditional woven baskets for shopping. The sign that appears behind the figures, "Vins et Degustation," advertises both wines and wine tastings. Each of the twenty districts of Paris has its fresh produce market, often three times a week, but none in the capital is as atmospheric as this.

Although the sign on the barrels to the left advertises "Vin Rouge," this little pavilion, on the corner of the rue Mouffetard and the rue du Pot de Fer, is actually a water fountain. The water spout can be seen just above ground level on the left. It was one of a series of fourteen, built in the 1620s in order to supply fresh water to Left Bank Parisians at a time when the usual source of drinking water was the Seine. The supply here comes from a Roman aqueduct restored to bring clean drinking water from outside Paris to the fountains of the Luxembourg gardens, which were being built for Queen Marie de Medici at the time.

The street name means "iron pot," which the locals would have used for fetching water from the fountain. Today this street is lined with bistros and inexpensive cafés. In the 1920s, George Orwell lived here while researching his novel *Down and Out in Paris and London*, a depiction of the seamier side of life. In the book he describes the irregular architecture of the street as "leprous houses, lurching at queer altitudes." Today we would call this "picturesque charm"! The fountain still provides a trickle of water today.

This shot shows the Odéon Métro station during the terrible floods of 1910 when most of the underground network was put out of action. The system was only a few years old at this time. The first line was opened in July 1900 in time for the Universal Exposition. The authorities needed a transport system suited to the number of visitors flocking into the city for the Universal Exhibition. Before the Métro, public transportation consisted of thirty-one tram lines, twenty-five bus routes, and 102 riverboats. The Odéon station takes its name from the famous theater nearby.

Today the majority of the Métro stations have changed little. Some have maintained their lovely art nouveau entrances by Hector Guimard, and most are still decorated with the characteristic white ceramic tiles with beveled edges that are made at Gien. The Gien factory on the Loire River is famous for its ceramics so fine that they resemble the quality of porcelain. The blue-and-white enameled name plaques in each station were introduced early on and are carefully located so that passengers can see the name of the station from wherever they are sitting in the train when it pulls in.

La Ruche (the beehive) was the name given to this rotunda built by Gustave Eiffel as a wine pavilion for the Universal Exhibition of 1900. The building is circular and divided into twelve pie-shaped segments. The main entrance, on the other side, opens into a circular hall with a freestanding wooden staircase giving access to the three floors. In 1902 the structure was purchased by the sculptor Alfred Boucher, dismantled, and reerected on this site in the fourteenth district. This area, which was not built up, was gradually being colonized by artists who could not afford the rents at Montparnasse. La Ruche became the eccentric home of many of these artists. There were as many as 140 studios in and around this building.

Boucher, who was a successful academic sculptor in his day, was a kind and benevolent patron to struggling artists. He gave the rooms at La Ruche to young artists, many of whom were Jewish and had come from central Europe to escape persecution. It was to become one of the foremost birthplaces of modernism, a veritable Mecca of modern art. Among the "bees" working at the hive were Fernand Léger, Constantin Brancusi, Michel Kikoine, and Ossip Zadkine. Modigliani was a frequent visitor and Chagall took a studio in 1910. Artists still live and work in this bohemian paradise today, paying a modest rent. The building is classified as a "historic monument" and belongs to the city of Paris.

The Hôtel de Sully is one of many beautiful mansions for which the Marais Quarter has become famous. The word *hôtel* here refers to a private town house or mansion. This palatial residence, built in 1624, belonged to the Duke of Sully, finance minister to Henry IV. The design of the house heralded a new age of comfortable living. Servants' quarters and stables were located on the noisy, smelly street side, with the main residential pavilion standing between a quiet courtyard and decorative garden. In the nineteenth century, the whole area declined into a poor district, and the house was disfigured by the addition of extra structures.

Today the building stands as one of the most prestigious of the Marais town houses. The parasite pavilion constructed between the two towers has been demolished, lightening the structure and restoring the elegant symmetry of the original façade. The house was one of the first to be restored in a campaign to revive this historic quarter beginning in the 1960s. Appropriately this is now the headquarters of the Historic Monuments Commission. The building has sumptuous interiors that are open to the public on National Heritage weekend, and in one of its rooms beneath the original painted-beam ceiling, there is a lovely bookstore specializing in the history of Paris.

This turreted castle is a rare example of civil medieval architecture in Paris. The house was originally built between 1480 and 1510 for the archbishop of the town of Sens in Burgundy, who was more important than the bishop of Paris. The house is built like a military castle, guarded by two round watchtowers and a gate with a portcullis, to protect the entrance to the courtyard behind. The triangular opening above the doorway was designed so that a vertical battering ram could be dropped on any assailant. In the early seventeenth century, the estranged wife of Henry IV, flamboyant Queen Margot, led a decadent life here. The painted sign above the door denotes that when this photograph was taken in the nineteenth century, the building had become a jelly factory.

In 1916 the building was bought as a ruin by the city of Paris. A long restoration program was then undertaken between 1936 and 1962. The round object stuck in the wall of the gable on the left is a cannonball, which became lodged here during the revolutionary uprising in 1830. This revolution caused the end of the old-style regime and ushered in the constitutional monarchy of King Louis Philippe. Today the building houses the Bibliothèque Forney, a library of decorative and fine arts used by the school of master craftsmen located nearby. The library consists of 150,000 volumes, 250,000 prints, a collection of wallpaper, designs for furniture, ironwork, and samples of eighteenth-century decoration.

The rue des Francs Bourgeois cuts through the Marais from east to west. In medieval times, a *franc bourgeois* was a person exempt from paying taxes because he was too poor. A *bourgeois* was someone who lived in the town, or *bourg*. In the 1350s a hostel was built here to house forty-eight such Parisians. The hostel gave its name to the road, but was renamed for the duration of the Revolution. The house with the elegant corbeled turret was built in 1510 for Jean Herouet, treasurer to Louis XII.

The domestic watchtower became very fashionable in this period. A beautifully sculpted turret was sure to be noticed as a clear sign of the prestige and status of the residents. Today the Maison Herouet has been completely rebuilt, an exact copy of the original that was destroyed as a result of the German bombardment in 1944. The liquor store has been replaced by a modern art gallery and the rue des Francs Bourgeois is today an elegant promenade of luxury shops, bars, cafés, and restaurants.

The rue François Miron was, before the building of the rue de Rivoli, the main road leading from the Bastille gate to the Louvre. This principal thoroughfare through the aristocratic neighborhood became the best address for those wanting to see and be seen, particularly when the royal parades and court processions passed by. In the seventeenth and eighteenth centuries, the road developed as a row of elegant houses. Number 82, seen here, is late Louis XIV–style. The window tops are slightly curved and the ironwork of the balcony is characteristic. The ground floor arcades consist of two stores, above which can be seen the semicircular windows of the shopkeepers' storerooms or apartments. The left arcade is the coaching entrance leading to the courtyard and stables behind.

Today the lovely mansions along this road have all been restored. The majority of these Paris buildings are made from the local stone, which is soft and must be delicately cleaned with steam and running water. Special resins are blended with powdered stone to make durable repairs to the sculptures. The details of the façade have been delicately restored, and the balcony is supported by decorative corbels, the central one being an exotic Moorish head wearing a turban. This building, one of many in the area acquired by the city, was bought in 1943, and today it is part of the Maison Européen de la Photographie.

The narrow rue des Rosiers is the main street of the Pletzl, the Jewish village of the Marais. This lovely street curves its way along, following inside the line of the twelfth-century city wall. Its name comes from the rose gardens planted here in medieval times when the land inside the city wall was a military no-man's land on which building was not permitted. This area attracted the poor Jewish immigrants in the nineteenth century who came here escaping persecution. Until World War II, the community here was mainly Ashkenazic, and people earned their living as tailors and skilled manual workers.

Today the street looks little changed—the façades of the buildings are recognizably the same. However, most of the original community was dispersed during the Occupation with a majority sent to perish in concentration camps. The Jewish community here today is principally Sephardic, from North Africa. There are several Jewish schools here, many synagogues—including one built by Hector Guimard in the art nouveau style—and many specialty stores and restaurants. The street is very popular for its foods and has become the place to find good bagels and falafel. One of its most celebrated addresses is the restaurant Jo Goldenberg's.

This ancient passageway is a perfectly preserved example of the architecture of a medieval street. The street is narrow and cobbled, with gutters on either side to channel the waste and sewage that would have been thrown from the openings of the overhanging stepped gables. In medieval times this alleyway was the back entrance into Queen Isabelle of Bavaria's country residence, where she carried out her romantic assignations. In 1407 her lover, the Duke of Orléans, who was also her brother-in-law, tried to slip away discreetly into the night along this passageway. He was brutally murdered by the henchmen of his enemy, the Duke of Burgundy.

Today the passage still carries its medieval name. The word *arbaletriers* means "crossbowmen," which refers to the soldiers, guardians of the nearby city wall, who would come here to practice their archery skills. The overhanging gables have surprisingly survived. The marketeers' wheelbarrows have been replaced by parked cars, but otherwise the street is little changed. It is surprisingly scruffy with graffiti for a street in an area that has recently undergone such a radical gentrification.

The Place des Vosges was built in the early seventeenth century as the first of a series of royal squares. This regal architectural ensemble is one of the first examples anywhere in Paris of town planning. A large area of the Marais was acquired by Henry IV and cleared, ready for the building of the four-sided square. The pavilions were built of an elegant blend of red brick and pale stone, with gray slate for the roof. There were nine houses on each side, each one a uniform four arcades wide. Each of the houses has its own courtyard behind and they all share a lovely view over the central garden. Originally the central pavilion on the north and south sides were respectively the Queen and the King's Pavilions, from which they could watch the ceremonies.

Today the square is still one of the most elegant addresses in Paris. The central gardens are open to the public and are a favorite with locals, young and old. The garden has fountains and lovely pollarded lime trees. These prestigious residences have always been the home of the wealthy and famous. This view is taken from in front of the house where Victor Hugo lived from 1832 to 1848, while working on *Les Miserables*. It is now the Hugo museum. On a summer's day crowds gather in the gardens to sunbathe and listen to the performers. Jazz bands and chamber orchestras provide quality music for all to enjoy.

This photograph shows the rue de Lyon during the terrible floods of 1910. At this time the whole of the capital was brought to a standstill. The Métro was put out of action between January and April 1910. Parisians moved about using temporary walkways and gangplanks to enable them to embark in rowboats. In the center of the city the water level had risen to twenty-seven feet. It is estimated that the flow of the Seine during the worst of the flood reached 3,100 cubic yards per second as opposed to forty cubic yards per second at its slowest. Plaques marking the flood level can be found throughout Paris.

Today the rue de Lyon, taking its name from the nearby Gare de Lyon, is a perfect example of nineteenth-century architecture. The uniformity, harmony, and symmetry of Haussmann's Paris is evident in the buildings, all six stories tall and the same height. In the nineteenth century, an Englishman, Arthur Saville-Grant, invented the kiosk, which he made a fortune selling in Paris.

The sidewalks soon became overcrowded with kiosks selling everything imaginable: souvenirs, newspapers, flowers, and lottery tickets. During the time of Haussmann, people complained that the overcrowding caused by kiosks was worse than before the city had been transformed. The sidewalks are still littered with them today.

The veneration of the Sacred Heart became popular at the end of the nineteenth century. This is when the seventeenth-century nun, Marguerite-Marie Alacoque, who had visions of Christ telling her to popularize the cult, was beatified. The famous church in Montmartre was built following the disastrous Franco-Prussian War, after which French Catholics vowed to raise money to build the massive church by popular subscription. Those who wished to donate could buy stones for the edifice according to a special tariff. Hidden stones were the cheapest, a visible stone carved with initials was a bit more expensive, and a pillar was only for the well-to-do. The National Assembly declared the project a state undertaking in 1873. The church was finally consecrated on October 16, 1919. It is built from a white stone that has the curious property of being self-cleaning where the rain has access to it, and it has consequently never needed to be cleaned.

Today the church is a favorite in Paris and the only one open twenty-four hours a day for the veneration of the Host. The building of the church was very complex. First the state had to negotiate with fourteen separate landowners to acquire the land, then because of the risk of subsidence due to the quarries, eighty-three foundation pillars, some forty-five yards deep, had to be constructed. It was recently estimated that six million visitors a year come to the church, half of whom are pilgrims. It is home to the biggest bell in the world, the Savoyarde. The views across Paris from the terrace are spectacular, and on a summer's evening, crowds gather with picnics, bottles of wine, and a few guitars to play in the sunset.

172 — PARIS. Le Moulin Rouge. ND Phot.

The Moulin Rouge was opened in 1886 as a rival to the successful dance hall the Moulin de la Galette, which was also a real working windmill on the hill of Montmartre. Joseph Oller and Charles Zidler's Moulin Rouge was an extravagant folly that would become internationally famous. It was an immediate success. The extraordinary décor created by the painter Adolphe Willette consisted of an immense garden with a Normandy-style thatched house, a Dutch windmill, a mock bullfighting ring, and, of course, at the main entrance, a huge windmill painted bright red. In the garden was a stage where famous dancers executed the now world-famous French cancan, which had been set to music by Offenbach. Next to the stage was a colossal stucco elephant from which the orchestra played for a troupe of belly dancers! Lautrec loved the color and ambience of the Moulin Rouge and painted many posters for the show featuring the famous dancers La Goulou and Jane Avril.

The original magic of the cabaret faded away during the two world wars, but in 1951 new life was breathed into the show by the dynamic Henri Mahé. The show has once again hit international fame with its colorful dinner revues. One can still see a French cancan danced with gusto alongside more traditional acts while sitting down to dinner or sipping Champagne. Each few seasons the revue is completely changed, and according to the mysterious rules of theater superstition, the name must always begin with an *F.* As can be seen in the photograph, taken at dusk as the city sheds its daylight persona to become Paris by night, the revue featured is "Féerie," (Fairy Tale). How appropriate for Montmartre, the most magical of Paris's one hundred villages.

VIEUX MONTMARTRE. — Au Bon Vin de chez Catherine
sur la Place du Tertre.

Cliché Duval

This café claims to have been founded in 1793, the year that Louis XVI and Marie Antoinette went to the guillotine. It is certainly one of the oldest cafés on the Butte Montmartre. This village outside Paris was well known for its cafés and cabarets. Situated outside the city walls, liquor and tobacco were cheaper, as the vendors did not have to pay the heavy taxes levied at the tollgates. Montmartre had its own vineyard, and although the quality of the wine was notoriously poor, it was cheap and flowed freely. The vineyard was saved from the developers by locals, and there is a grape-picking festival every year, which is very popular with Parisians and tourists alike. The wine is now an expensive curiosity.

Today the Maison Catherine, now known as La Mére Catherine, is one of many cafés around the square that cater to the thousands of visitors who come to see the artists at work and visit the Sacré Coeur. It is said that the word *bistrot* entered the French language here! After the fall of Napoleon, Russian soldiers who were billeted here frequented this café and called out "bistrot bistrot." It was thought they were demanding coffee, but in fact the expression means "quickly, quickly." Often the bars were simply merchants of daily necessities such as wood or coal, who sold coffee or a glass of wine to their customers. In the little bars of Montmartre, it is likely that more wine was drunk than coffee.

The picturesque Place du Tertre has always been the heart of the village of Montmartre. Here in 1904 the square is frequented by a few locals and surrounded by small houses, with a few cafés and stores. It was the financial misfortunes of the abbey, which had once owned nearly all the hill, that enabled this quarter to develop as a residential village. As the years went by the abbey had to sell off its land, enabling the villagers to move in. Several plaques around the square remind us of its history. At number 19, the Free Commune was set up in the 1920s to perpetuate the traditions of the village. At number 21, the plaque tells us that in 1898 Louis Renault drove a gasoline-powered automobile of his own invention to the top of the hill, despite predictions that it would never get him there.

Nowadays the square is one of the most frequented in Paris. It is delightfully pretty and maintains the tradition of painters creating their works here in Montmartre. Some two hundred artists stand at their easels selling oil paintings and watercolor views of Paris. Portraitists abound, touting for customers. You may have a flattering portrait painted, a caricature drawn in charcoal, or a silhouette deftly cut out of black paper. In the center of the square, the café owners have established a massive open-air terrace where one can dine in the magical atmosphere in the long summer evenings to the traditional tunes of the accordion.

Place Blanche was once a gateway into Paris on the old tollhouse walls. *Blanche* means "white," and it refers back to the days when Montmartre was quarried for its gypsum to make plaster. The gypsum was dried in kilns and ground down by the windmills, which used to crown the hill of Montmartre. The road that climbs the hill to the left, rue Lepic, was built to enable the carts to bring the gypsum down toward Paris. The plaster spilled off the carts and the road and square were literally white. At the corner of the rue Lepic, a sign attached to a lamppost advertises the Moulin de la Galette dance hall, where some thirty years previously, Renoir had painted his famous canvas now in the Musée d'Orsay.

Today the architecture of the square is remarkably similar. There are no longer any windmills here. The quarrying of plaster in Montmartre was banned around 1900, when so much of the material had been removed that the village was suffering from subsidence. The quarries were called the "Quarries of America" because so much of the plaster was exported to the U.S. Today the square is a parking lot for hundreds of tourist buses whose clients come to stroll along toward Place Pigalle to admire the neon lights, most of which are red!

This wonderfully evocative photograph shows two artists at work behind the famous Moulin de la Galette. The windmill had once been a working mill that ground the locally grown grain. The word *galette* refers to the flat wheat cakes, similar to modern-day crèpes, that were made from the flour produced here. As the area became urbanized and the mill redundant with the advent of modern technology, it was converted into a simple cabaret. The owners built a viewing stage on its roof and a dance platform in its garden. The cabaret was far from sophisticated, furnished with simple wooden benches and tables and serving quantities of the local wine. It nevertheless became extremely popular, and bourgeois Parisians would come and dance a frenzied polka alongside the factory workers and concierges.

The mill exists today, but the cabaret is long gone. It can no longer be seen from the same angle. What had been everyman's Paris at the turn of the century was to become in the 1920s the private homes and gardens of a bohemian elite. The modern house to the right was built for the kindly artist Francisque Poulbot, who had made a name and a fortune painting the street urchins and ragamuffins of Montmartre. He used his fortune to found a dispensary and orphanage for the local children, which still exists. More or less next door is the private mansion of the surrealist Tristan Zara, whose avant-garde cubist villa was built by the modernist architect Adolf Loos.

At the end of the nineteenth century this picturesque collection of buildings stood at the top of the rue Lepic. The tall house was the clinic of Dr. Blanche from 1820 to 1847. He specialized in treating mental disorders among artists and writers, creating an alternative to the terrible conditions in the asylums of the day. Among his famous patients were the poet Gerard de Nerval and the writer Maupassant. Modigliani lived for a while in the little house to the far left. The octagonal tower on the right was built as a water tower in 1835 and elegantly decorated in the neo-Renaissance style popular at the time.

The view is much changed today. Dr. Blanche moved his clinic to the village of Passy later in the century to a beautiful residence next to Balzac's house, which the author had dreamed of buying for his aristocratic lover Mme. Hanska. The reservoir has been modified, its water container removed when the new water tower and colossal reservoirs were built next to Sacré Coeur in 1877. The pretty neo-Renaissance pavilion beneath remains and has been converted into an office. Its façade is still adorned with a curious cockleshell-shaped grotto, framing an urn surrounded by water nymphs, an allusion to the original purpose of the tower.

In September of 1870, Paris was besieged by the Prussians. The hilltop of Montmartre was always a strategic point from which to observe and defend the city. After terrible suffering and starvation caused by the siege, the Parisians were angry to learn of the government's signing of a disastrous treaty followed by some insensitive measures that inflamed the poor. On March 18, 1871, at 4:30 A.M., the government launched a massive operation to recuperate the cannons that had stood on the hill to defend the city during the siege. Hostile Parisians refused to give up the artillery to the army. By 8:30 A.M. all was lost for the government, who then fled to Versailles. The 171 cannons needed 850 horses to remove them. This incident was the starting point of the Paris Commune.

Today, standing at the top of this famous *butte*, or hill, it is clear why this was such an important military position. Napoleon had investigated the hill when it was outside the city and had ordered a road to be built here (rue Lepic) to give the army access, if necessary; the Cossaks were later billeted here for the same reason. The views across the capital are simply stunning. The skyline to the horizon has somewhat changed, with the two dominant landmarks being the Eiffel Tower and the Montparnasse Tower, a fifty-two-story skyscraper. Here, one is about 450 feet above the city. The view can be made even more spectacular by climbing into the dome of Sacré Coeur.

INDEX

Abelard, Pierre 96
Aga Khan 83
Alacoque, Marguerite-Marie 128
Alphand, Jean Charles 5
Alsace 12, 36
American Embassy 11
Amsterdam 35
Angelina's 55
Arc de Triomphe 6, 7, 9, 24
architectural revolution 28
Argenteuil 32
Armistice Day 7
art deco 37, 50
art nouveau 109, 121
Atget, Eugène 5
Aulenti, Gae 93
Austerlitz, Battle of 20
Auteuil 62
Avril, Jane 130

Balzac, Honoré de 62, 63, 141
Bardet 58
Bastille 118
Bastille Day 9
Bastille Square 23
Baudelaire 99
Bay of Cadiz 58
Belgrand, Eugene 5
Belle Époque 55
Bergundy 114
Bergundy, Duke of 122
Bernhardt, Sarah 39
Berton, rue 62, 63
Bibliothèque Forney 115
Bièvre River 104
Bird Market 76, 77
Blanche, Dr. 140, 141
Blanche, Place 136, 137
Blondel, Fraïnçois 30
Bonaparte, Napoleon 6, 7, 8, 20, 40, 54, 89, 133, 143
Bordeaux 14
Boucher, Alfred 110, 111
Bouquinistes 74, 75
Bourse du Commerce 48, 49
Brancusi, Constantin 111
Brussels 35
Butte Montmartre 132, 142, 143

cancan 27, 130, 131
Carilingian 5
Carrefour de Buci 100, 101
Catacombs 42
Chagall, Marc 23, 111
Chaillot 62
Chaillot hill 57, 58
Chamber of Commerce 49
Champ de Mars 57
Champs Elysées 8, 9, 16, 54
Channel Tunnel 33
charnel house 42
Chartres 57
Châtelet 46
Châtelet Monument 40, 41
Chopin, Frederic 24
Citroën 64, 65
Citroën, André 64
Clément, Gilles 65
Clichy 64

Clignancourt 75
Cognacq, Ernest 51
Collette 95
Cologne 89
Conciergerie 72, 73
Concorde St. Lazare 33
Convent des Capucines 27
Corday, Charlotte 98
Cordeliers 98
Cour de Rohan 94, 95
Credit Municipale 52
Crimea 60
Crown of Thorns 69

Dante 84
Danton, George-Jacques 89, 98
David 89
Davioud, Gabriel 38, 58
D-Day 102
de Bièvre, rue 84, 85, 97
de Brosse, Salomon 88
de Constantin, rue 86, 87
de Gaulle, Charles 14
de la Cité, Île 72, 76, 77, 86
de la Concorde, Place 8, 10, 11, 12, 34, 54
de la Révolution, Place 10
de la Verrerie, rue 47
de l'Alma, Pont 60, 61
de l'École de Médecine, rue 98, 99
de l'Etoile, Place 8
de l'Europe, Place 32
de l'Opera, Place 27
de Lutèce, rue 86, 87
de Lyon, rue 126, 127
de Nerval, Gerard 140
de Rivoli, rue 47, 54, 55, 118
de Rome, rue 32
de Sebastopol, boulevard 41
Degas, Edgar 80
d'Eglantine, Fabre 89
des Capucines, boulevard 26, 27
des Francs Bourgeois, rue 116, 117
des Innocents, Place 42, 43
des Rats, rue 69
des Rosiers, rue 120, 121
des Ursins, Jean Juvenal 82
des Ursins, rue 82, 83
des Vosges, Place 124, 125
Descartes, Rene 102
Descartes, rue 102, 103
Desmoulins, Camille 89, 98
Diana, Princess 21
Diane de Poitiers 94
Dickens, Charles 33
Drouet, Juliette 13
du Faubourg St. Denis, rue 30, 31
du Pot de Fer, rue 106, 107
du Tertre, Place 134, 135

École de Médecine, 98
Edward VII, King 8, 56
Egypt 11, 40
Eiffel, Gustav 56, 110
Eiffel Tower 6, 56, 57, 64, 143
Elba 6
Erasmus 96
Etat Français 14
Europe 34, 111
Eurostar 35

Fauré, Gabrile 24
Fete du Pain, La 71
floods, 1658 81
floods, 1910 108, 126
Florence 88
Fontaine, Pierre-François 55
Fouquet, Jean 82
François Miron, rue 118, 119
Franco-Prussian War 12, 70, 128
Frédéric Sauton, rue 68, 69
Free Commune 134
French Navy 11, 15
French Revolution 5, 16, 17, 27, 38, 42, 66, 73, 89, 98, 115, 116

Gabriel, Jacques 13
Galleries Lafayette 28, 29
Gare de l'Est 31, 36, 37
Gare de Lyon 127
Gare d'Orsay 92, 93
Gare du Nord 33, 34, 35
Gare St. Lazare 32, 33
Garnier, Charles 22, 23, 104
Germany 14, 55, 59, 117
Gien 109
Giverny 32
Gothic 46
Guimard, Hector 109, 121

Hanska, Mme. 141
Haussmann, Baron Georges 5, 18, 19, 22, 34, 46, 86, 127
Haussmann, boulevard 29
Hemingway, Ernest 103
Henry II, King 16, 94
Henry III, King 52
Henry IV, King 20, 52, 88, 112, 114, 124
Henry of Navarre 18
Herouet, Jean 116, 117
Historic Monuments Commission 113
Hitler, Adolf 14, 55, 56
Hittorf, Jacques-Ignace 34, 35
Hôtel Crillon 11, 15
Hôtel de Sens 114, 115
Hôtel de Sully 112, 113
Hôtel de Ville 19, 36, 54, 70, 71, 75
Hôtel des 2 Lions 83
Hôtel Dieu 86
Hotel Meurice 55
Hugo, Victor 13, 66, 90, 125
Huguenots 18
Hunchback of Notre Dame, The 66, 71

industrial revolution 5
Isabelle, Queen of Bavaria 122
Italy 54, 88, 93

Jay, Louise 51
Jo Goldenberg's 121
John, Augustus 94
Jourdain, Frantz 50
Joyce, James 103

Kikoine, Michel 111
kiosk 127

La Galou 130
La Môme Phémie 46
La Ruche 110, 111

Lalanne, Claude 45
Lalanne, François-Xavier 45
Latin Quarter 5, 69, 94, 96, 103
l'Automobile-Club de France 11
Lautrec, Toulouse 76, 130
Leclerc, General Jacque-Philippe 14
Left Bank 60, 68, 75, 79, 82, 100, 105
Léger, Fernand 111
Lepic, rue 136, 140, 141, 143
Leroux, Gaston 22
Les Halles market 42, 44, 45
Levallois 64
Loire River 109
London 33, 35
Loos, Adolf 139
Lorraine 12, 36
Louis Philippe, King 13, 115
Louis, XII, King 116
Louis, XIII, King 89
Louis XIV, King 30, 100, 118
Louis XVI, King 10, 16, 20
Louvre 8, 16, 17, 19, 54, 72, 75, 82, 88, 118
Luxembourg Gardens 90, 91, 106
Luxembourg Palace 88, 89

Madeleine Church 11, 24, 25
Mahé, Henri 131
Maison Catherine, La 132, 132
Maison Européenne de la Photographie 119
Maître Albert 96, 97
Mansart, Jules Hardouin 20
Marais Quarter 51, 112, 113, 116, 120, 124
Marat, Jean-Paul 98
Margaret, Princess 18
Margot, Queen 114
Marie Antoinette 10, 16, 73, 132
Marie, Christophe 81
Marie, Pont 80, 81
Marly 8
Marville, Charles 5
Maubert 69
Maubert, Place 85
Maupassant, Guy de 140
Maxim's 15
Mayor of Paris 71
Medici, Queen Catherine de 16
Medici, Queen Marie de 48, 88, 89, 106
Merovingian 5
Métro 33, 35, 108, 109, 126
Ministère de la Marine 14, 15
Mitterand, President 85, 97
modernism 111
Modigliani, Amedeo 111, 140
Monet, Claude 32, 78
Montmartre 128, 130, 131, 134, 135, 136, 137, 139
Montparnasse 110, 143
Montparnasse Tower 143
Mouffetard, rue 104, 105
Moulin de la Galette 130, 136, 138, 139
Moulin Rouge 130, 131
Musée Cognacq-Jay 51
Musée de la Marine 59
Musée des Monuments Français 59
Musée d'Orsay 136

Nadar 38
Napoleon III, Emperor 5, 36, 54, 60, 74, 79
National Assembly 128

Neuf, Pont 50, 52, 53, 74
Normandy 14, 32, 33, 94, 102
North Africa 121
Notre Dame Cathedral 66, 67, 79, 82

Odéon Métro Station 108, 109
Offenbach, Jacques 27, 130
Oller, Joseph 130
Orient Express 37
Orléans, Duke of 122
Orwell, George 103, 107
Ossip, Zadkine 111

Palais de Chaillot 58, 59
Palais de Justice 86
Palm Fountain 40
Paris Commune 12, 17, 20, 21, 70, 142
Paris Opera 22, 23, 39, 104
Passage des Arbaletriers 122, 123
Passy 62, 141
Pei, I. M. 17
Percier, Charles 55
Pétain, Marshal 14
Petit Pont 78, 79
Piaf, Edith 46
Pigalle, Place 137
Pitti Palace 88
Pletzl 120
Pouillon, Fernand 83
Poulbot, Francisque 139
Pradier, James 13
Préfecture de Police 87
Printemps 29
Provost, Alain 65
Prussia 12, 142

Qai des Grands Augustins 52
Queen's Garden 16

Renaissance 43, 48
Renault, Louis 134
Renoir, Pierre Auguste 136
Resistance, the 56
Rhineland 30
Right Bank 75, 80
Ritz Hotel 21
Rivoli 54
Rodin, Auguste 104
Roman Empire 6
Rome 5, 20, 58, 92, 106
Rothschilds 32
Rouen 94
Rubens, Peter Paul 88
Ruggieri 48
Russia 59, 133

Sacré Coeur 128, 129, 132, 141, 143
St. Bartholomew massacre 18
St. Bon 47
St. Bon, rue 46, 47
St. Denis Arch 30
St. Denis, Church of 30
St. Eustache, Church of 48
St. Geneviève, hill of 102
St. Germain 100
St. Germain, boulevard 95
St. Germain-en-Lay 32
St. Germain l'Auxerrois, Church of 18, 19
St. Helena 6

Saint-Louis, Île 75, 80
St. Médard 104
Saint Médard, Place 104, 105
St. Médéric, Church of 46, 47
St. Michel fountain 38
St. Michel, Pont 78, 79
St. Ouen 64
Saint-Saëns, Camille 24, 94
Samaritaine, la 50, 51
Sauvage, Henri 50
Saville-Grant, Arthur 127
Seine River 5, 22, 50, 61, 70, 78, 79, 80, 83, 84, 85, 100, 105, 126
Sénat 89
Sens 114
Siege of Paris 12
Sorbonne 103
statue of Strasbourg 12, 13
Strasbourg 12, 13, 36
Sully, Duke of 112
surrealist 74, 139

Théâtre du Châtelet 38, 39
Théâtre Nationale de Chaillot 59
Third Republic 14, 21
Tour de France 9
Tour St. Jacques 54
Tribunal de Commerce 73, 87
Trocadero 58
Tuileries gardens 9
Tuileries Palace 16, 17, 70

Universal Exhibition, 1855 36, 60
Universal Exhibition, 1878 58
Universal Exhibition, 1889 56
Universal Exhibition, 1900 92, 108, 110
Universal Exhibition, 1937 59
Universal Exposition, 1900 33

Valois 18
Varennes 16
Vendôme, Place 20, 21, 24
Verdun 37
Verlaine, Paul 102, 103
Verne, Jules 38
Versailles 19, 100, 142
Vetheuil 78
Vichy 14
Victoria, avenue 36
Victoria, Queen 19, 36
Viollet-le-Duc, Eugene 67
von Choltitz, General Dietrich 14, 55

Washington Monument 56
Wilette, Adolphe 130
World War I 7, 10, 37
World War II 49, 97, 120

Zara, Tristan 139
Zidler, Charles 130
Zola, Émile 44
Zouave 61